CRYSTALS & CHAKRAS

••• An Oracle Deck for Inner Balance •••

978 4046711475

U.S. Games Systems, Inc.
179 Ludlow Street
Stamford, CT 06902 USA
www.usgamesinc.com

Publisher
Balthazar Pagani

Editing
Caterina Grimaldi

Drafting
PEPE nymi

Graphic design
Davide Canesi / PEPE nymi

Vivida

Vivida® trademark is the property of White Star s.r.l.
www.vividabooks.com

© 2023 White Star s.r.l.
Piazzale Luigi Cadorna, 6
20123 Milano, Italy
www.whitestar.it

Translation: TperTradurre s.r.l., Rome
Editing: Phillip Gaskill

All rights reserved. No part of this publication may be
reproduced, stored in a retrieval system, or transmitted
in any form or by any means, including electronic,
mechanical, photocopying, recording, or otherwise,
without written permission from the publisher.

Made in China

CRYSTALS & CHAKRAS

••• An Oracle Deck for Inner Balance •••

Written by
Luca Apicella

Illustrations by
Alessandra De Cristofaro

CONTENTS

•••

INTRODUCTION

7

HOW TO USE THIS DECK

8

THE CARDS

Black Tourmaline 14	Garnet...........................19
Black Onyx 15	Petrified Wood............ 20
Black Obsidian 16	Chiastolite Andalusite..21
Red Jasper.....................17	Orange Calcite.............22
Ruby................................18	Carnelian 23

Sunstone	24
Pyrite	25
Tiger's Eye	26
Yellow and Honey Calcite	27
Yellow Fluorite	28
Citrine Quartz	29
Rhodochrosite	30
Lepidolite	31
Rose Quartz	32
Malachite	33
Emerald	34
Green Aventurine	35
Lapis Lazuli	36
Sodalite	37
Blue Chalcedony	38
Aquamarine	39
Angelite	40
Azurite	41
Sugilite	42
Purple Fluorite	43

Amethyst	44
Ametrine	45
Magnesite	46
White Onyx	47
Moonstone	48
Selenite	49
Hyaline Quartz	50
First Chakra	51
Second Chakra	52
Third Chakra	53
Fourth Chakra	54
Fifth Chakra	55
Sixth Chakra	56
Seventh Chakra	57
Stone Cleansing	58
Aura Cleansing	59
Messages	60
Energy Vampire	61
Feminine Principle	62
Masculine Principle	63

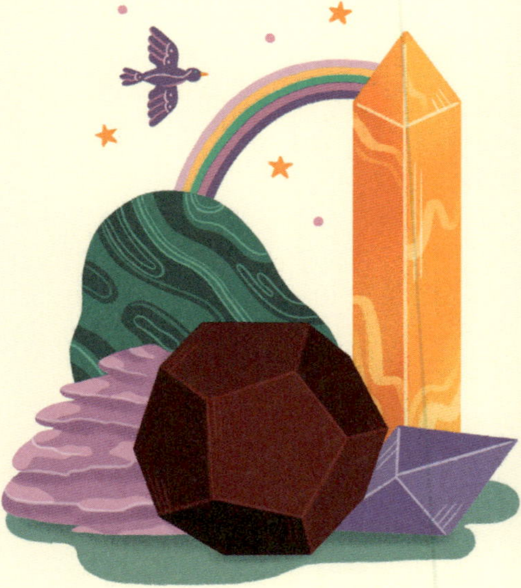

INTRODUCTION

◆ ◆ ◆

We are constantly surrounded and affected by frequencies. Altering frequencies can cause our body, emotions, mind and spirit to show symptoms that can then turn into disease. Some holistic disciplines consider stones as powerful allies in remedying these imbalances, recognizing their ability to lend their frequencies to help people heal.

The images contained in these cards skillfully summarize the messages of the relevant stones. And just like the stones, the cards representing them can also aid us in the small and big decisions we have to make every day. They are a source of inspiration when we need a silent guide to communicate with us deeply and help us awaken in the morning with fresh ideas. Observe the cards for a few minutes: their message will rise from the unconscious to the light of consciousness. This oracle is a collection of those stones that I consider most helpful for current times. Together with the seven chakra cards, this deck includes six "helper cards" to guide and interpret the answers of the oracle.

Listen in silence to your interior being; allow yourself the necessary time to explore the messages and allow your intuition to guide your use of this deck. Never stop searching; find your very own solution, that personal answer that—I hope—will then be able to lead you to other questions.

◆ ◆ ◆

HOW TO USE THIS DECK

◆ ◆ ◆

To explore a wide range of topics, use the cards to ask yourself questions, or consult the oracle with those you care about.

Each card also highlights the connection between a given crystal and its associated chakra, and provides applicable advice within the message contained. Try to also read the messages in the opposite way. It is written in *The Emerald Tablets of Thoth the Atlantean* that opposing extremes share

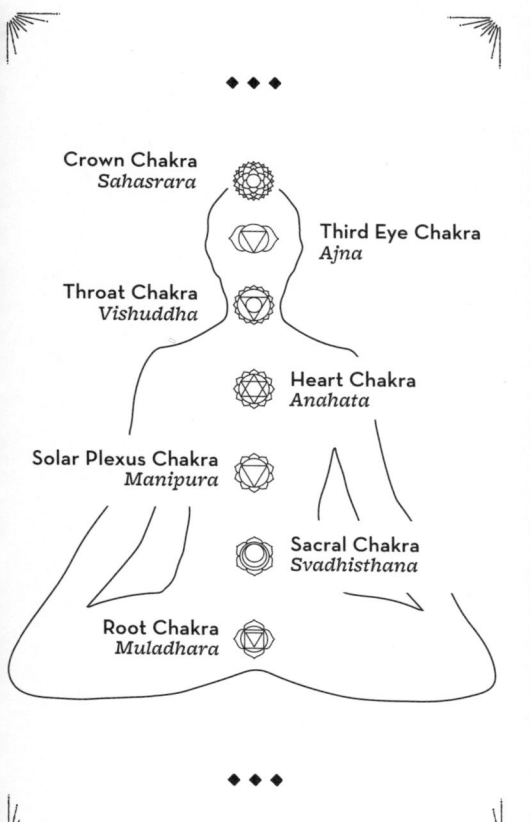

- Crown Chakra — *Sahasrara*
- Third Eye Chakra — *Ajna*
- Throat Chakra — *Vishuddha*
- Heart Chakra — *Anahata*
- Solar Plexus Chakra — *Manipura*
- Sacral Chakra — *Svadhisthana*
- Root Chakra — *Muladhara*

a common root, and this reading will help you trace it, allowing you to easily find the answer to your question.

Relax and then shuffle the cards as you ask your question. Lay them out from left to right and let your hand gravitate over the card for you. Choose and turn over one card at a time. Observe carefully and embrace the messages it conveys to you. The following guidelines will help you get the most information from the cards. Your own intuition will enhance the readings.

SINGLE CARD READING
For a single card personal reading, ask your question, then choose a card.

THREE CARD SPREAD
Choose three cards and place them in front of you.

The first, on the left, shows the way: the situation you are coming from, your past.

The second, in the middle, indicates your current situation.

The third, based on where you are at the moment, will guide you toward a possible future.

HOME SPREAD

Two cards for the floor portray your roots and emotions. The card to the left highlights your feminine energy and the past; to the right, your masculine energy and the present.

Two cards represent the walls, highlighting support, your borders with the world. To the left with your interior world; to the right with your exterior world.

Two cards symbolize the roof or your spiritual side. The card to the left represents your inner self; the one to your right is what you show to the world.

The last card signifies the entrance or exit, representing intuition or the remedy, to be interpreted depending on the question.

Note

The crystals highlighted in the cards may also be worn if you have them available. In this case, only wear one crystal at a time, the one you consider most appropriate for your question. Also remember that the stones should not be worn overnight or more than 21 days in a row. Moreover, remove the stones if you feel a sense of unease after two days. If this happens, ask yourself if you are truly ready for the proposed change.

THE CARDS

Black Tourmaline

Chakra:
Root Chakra / *Muladhara*

Color:
Black

Keyword:
Cleanse

Black tourmaline is an elongated and grooved crystal. Stones with such a structure are effective for the absorption and drainage of some types of energy. The potential of this stone is expressed toward electromagnetic energy, which is absorbed and in part drained away by electronic devices. Black tourmaline is effective in rooting to the earth when one is going through a difficult moment or managing intense events.

The oracle: *There is no point in running away, this is the world now. Don't lose sight of my persuasive darkness; it leads you down, it takes root in earthly vibrations.*

Black Onyx

Chakra:
Root Chakra / *Muladhara*

Color:
Black

Keyword:
Change

Black onyx has been known since ancient times. Where there's onyx, there's tenacity, the ability to "do what must be done." It can push you to be determined, even when uncomfortable action must be taken. In life's more difficult moments, onyx transmits stability and a sense of being rooted in the earth, allowing us to face even the most emotionally complicated moments.

The oracle: *I protect you from laziness; I lead you to action, to face the greatest challenges, to defend the weakest with the strength of a sword. Go and take action. Stay in the light.*

Black Obsidian

Chakra:
Root Chakra / *Muladhara*

Color:
Black

Keyword:
Grounding

Obsidian is a natural glass formed by volcanic gas. Like a volcano, it promotes the reemergence of emotions in a powerful way so that we can transform them from the dark and nebulous side to the bright and evolved side. It promotes rooting in those people who struggle to keep their feet on the ground, anchored to reality, with a tendency toward instability.

The oracle: *I bring out the unexpected in an assertive and powerful way. Maybe it scares you a little, and maybe it attracts you. Now, you can see your shadow side, made up of what you need to change about yourself.*

Red Jasper

Chakra:
Root Chakra / *Muladhara*

Color:
Red

Keyword:
Courage

The energy of red jasper allows the body to function in a general sense. We can identify this jasper as reawakened fire, which can shake up our lives to move us away from stagnant situations we are struggling to escape. It is a powerful protector against energy "vampires," people who have little energy and take it from those around them.

The oracle: *Fear doesn't break me. I resist, I do not break; I continue to be imperturbable.*

Ruby

Chakra:
Root Chakra / *Muladhara*

Color:
Red

Keyword:
Passion

Ruby is used in crystal therapy as an activator of basic energy, with an important focus on sexual energy. It activates the libido, especially male, but also female. Like all red stones, it affects one's fundamental nature, which refers to the basic emotions related to food (hunger), reproduction (sex), and survival (aggression). It stimulates the first chakra, increasing physical, emotional and mental energy.

The oracle: *It is possible to get lost amidst the flames, to cloak oneself with animal instincts. Or, choose the path of the heart, where the fire warms, and sexuality chases a new name: love. The choice is yours, human.*

Garnet

Chakra:
Root Chakra / *Muladhara*

Color:
Red

Keyword:
Energy

At first glance, garnet can appear almost black and opaque. However, placing it in the light will make it shine! Its famous red color glows, warming the eyes and heart. And yes, garnet is a producer of heat and thus fire in large quantities. When we are very tired and feel like we have no more energy, garnet is ready to stimulate the adrenal glands, producing cortisol and reserve energy.

The oracle: *I awake on fire, burning like lava. Your fangs get stronger. Hear my aggressive growls. You may perceive me as long-forgotten energy. Life resumes, with the present challenges—to win.*

Petrified Wood

Chakra:
Sacral Chakra / *Svadhisthana*

Color:
Brown

Keyword:
Melt

Speaking about petrified wood as a stone is not accurate; it is technically a fossil. There are a number of root stones, and this is one of the most powerful. Petrified wood helps us perform the most challenging actions by finding the right energy. One interesting quality is that when it is paired with azurite, it assists regressions to past lives.

The oracle: *Have you ever seen a rigid tree? I am now quartz, but I remember my flexibility perfectly. I can help you to break the crystallizations that have kept you stuck.*

Chiastolite Andalusite

Chakra:
Sacral Chakra / *Svadhisthana*

Color:
Brown

Keyword:
Protection

Chiastolite is just a variety of andalusite. At first glance, it makes an immediate impression due to its unique rhombic shape with a cross in the center. It is used for protection, especially when there is strong disharmonic energy to be addressed, to prevent it from damaging the people it meets. It particularly benefits the solar plexus, which also physically helps us relax at times when anxiety is very high.

The oracle: *My experience is ancient, linked to the cross. I embody it, leading you into the depths of the earth, on the journey where the shaman ventures. I protect you from any dense and dark energies, preventing you from getting lost.*

Orange Calcite

Chakra:
Sacral Chakra / *Svadhisthana*

Color:
Orange

Keyword:
Elaboration

The orange color of this calcite is beautiful, intense and very warm. It acts on the second chakra, which is weakened when it is subjected to considerable stress or to trauma of great impact. A problematic second chakra tends to send the third one off its axis. Orange calcite helps awaken the second chakra, thus aligning also the third one, which manages external influences.

The oracle: *Among swollen waters brimming with electric emotions, I find order. There, in your gut, emotions are processed, so you don't feel overwhelmed by the chaos of the world. Listen to yourself.*

Carnelian

Chakra:
Sacral Chakra / *Svadhisthana*

Color:
Orange

Keyword:
Feel

Carnelian agate is connected to the physical organs that are related to the processing of water. The organ it affects the most is the intestine. We should always remember that the intestine, on a deep and symbolic level, processes and absorbs emotions. Therefore, the use of carnelian is clear: it helps us embrace emotions by allowing us to deeply process them, transforming them into thoughts that don't remain in the mind but are consumed and metabolized, fostering profound change.

The oracle: *Let the gut guide the head, let the emotions be digested through rebirth.*

Sunstone

Chakra:
Sacral Chakra / *Svadhisthana* and Solar Plexus Chakra / *Manipura*

Color:
Orange

Keyword:
Self-esteem

Sunstone, with its golden reflections, is reminiscent of the star it gets its name from. It is an interesting bridge between the two energy points of the second and third chakras; it brings openness and sunshine. It encourages the second chakra to open the personal, internalized power located in the gut. It invites us to bloom, moving this energy to the third chakra to reveal it to the world, transforming personal power into power for the benefit of the community.

The oracle: *I can lead you to another way of life. I help you where your fears dwell, which are stagnant waters, swamps. Are you ready? Dare to do it! Your self-esteem will allow it!*

Pyrite

Chakra:
Solar Plexus Chakra / *Manipura*

Color:
Yellow

Keyword:
I understand

Pyrite is an excellent drainer of bodily fluids that contain the emotions we must now let go of. It increases the fire element, making you more reactive. If you wear pyrite, the answer will come suddenly in the form of a thought, an event or an encounter. In short, life will offer the answer, making you sigh a breath of relief and say "Now I get it!" It simply makes us notice the reason, without any emotional involvement; it just shows us the cause.

The oracle: *Foolish is he who seeks gold outside himself before shining inside, shedding light on his own dark, unseen part. I illuminate your fears so that you can observe them and rid yourself of them, dissolving them.*

Tiger's Eye

Chakra:
Solar Plexus Chakra / *Manipura*

Color:
Golden brown

Keyword:
Power

When we talk about tiger's eye, we immediately think of its gold-colored reflections. It is actually a powerful quartz that enhances focus on the details of a situation. Therefore, it is a highly recommended stone in circumstances in which a high level of attention is required. It boosts self-esteem, increasing self-confidence. Joy thus takes hold, bestowing greater lightness and the courage to face events in which one hesitates.

The oracle: *I help you in precise work, in meticulous processes, in the smallest details. You are surrounded by many different types of energy: I protect you from the most dangerous ones.*

Yellow and Honey Calcite

Chakra:
Solar Plexus Chakra / *Manipura*

Color:
Yellow

Keywords:
I shine again

This calcite in particular is good at calming the mind that generates anxiety. It bestows the lucidity and tranquility needed to act and thus prevents anxiety from devouring us. Confusion tends to subside, allowing us to find a quick solution to problems. Tensions in the physical, mental and spiritual body diminish, and sleep increases its restorative function.

The oracle: *I give you the power to be yourself, aligned and present. I am masculine energy: powerful and balanced. I help you find the right space between the mind and emotions.*

Yellow Fluorite

Chakra:
Solar Plexus Chakra / *Manipura*

Color:
Yellow

Keyword:
Transformation

Yellow fluorite is lined with shades of green or brown. Contrasting it with the light, it is as if the yellow color, representing the mental aspect, is pierced by the green, the reigning color of the heart chakra. This stone is useful for people who tend to analyze daily events in a cold and rational way. It helps them to enter a mode of emotional listening in which a frozen mind gives way to the heart.

The oracle: *Nothing can be considered perfect, and not everything can find an answer. I dissolve excessive rationality in favor of the heart, which warmly embraces your wise instincts.*

Citrine Quartz

Chakra:
Solar Plexus Chakra / *Manipura*

Color:
Yellow

Keyword:
Positivity

The attitude of this quartz, and of most yellow stones, is that of the "half-full glass," as it adds optimism to our view of life. In daily life, things happen that test our stability. Citrine quartz encourages us to find the good in events, reminding us that nothing happens randomly; everything is meant to teach us something. Therefore, in life's events, there's always a lesson to learn to improve ourselves.

The oracle: *I can help you when your light is tired. Your solar plexus shines, your finer energies shine. It is rare to see a star that stops shining: so shine! You can do it!*

Rhodochrosite

Chakra:
Heart Chakra / *Anahata*

Color:
Pink

Keyword:
Space for the new

Rhodochrosite is a difficult stone to manage. It helps when the emotions in the heart chakra are stagnant and you need to let them go. Rhodochrosite is a very powerful stone, forcing us to let emotions go at all costs, by hook or by crook. Rhodochrosite pushes us out of our comfort zone so that new emotions can arise to be felt and lived. It leads to confrontation so that our truth and love may surface.

The oracle: *I allow rebirth, but are you ready to let go? Are you ready to give up your old ways and welcome the new? There are new ways in this wonderful life. Have the courage to see them!*

Lepidolite

Chakra:
Heart Chakra / *Anahata* and Third Eye Chakra / *Ajna*

Color:
Pinkish Purple

Keyword:
Rest

This is a stone that calm the entire nervous system and allows you to maintain a connection with your intuition and thus accesses its maximum potential. When stability is fluctuating but not chronically, lepidolite helps stabilize the mood. It calms agitation and, in cases of disturbed sleep, allows for a restorative night.

The oracle: *I sedate your electric nerves, your heart calms down. Calm finally comes, and I invite you to slow down. I caress you so that you are not afraid. And together, hand in hand, we face the storm. Yes, the waves will be high, but your heart does not fear them. The night will be happier.*

Rose Quartz

Chakra:
Heart Chakra / *Anahata*

Color:
Pink

Keyword:
Nurture

Events like mourning, loss, or simply the desire to be consoled find refuge in this quartz. The heart is nothing more than a great cleanser, which, like a blast furnace, cleans the emotions we feel and then sends them as vehicles of information to the physical and energetic body. One important thing to note: since quartz is a very powerful stone, it shouldn't be worn for more than five consecutive days, followed by a five-day break.

The oracle: *I soften your torment, like a mother's hand, a father's embrace that calms you. It's time to stand and slowly let your pain flow away. I warm your heart. Let's wait for better times together.*

Malachite

Chakra:
Heart Chakra / *Anahata*

Color:
Green

Keywords:
Beauty

Malachite is a stone linked to femininity. It brings beauty and sensuality with its round and harmonious shapes. It helps process strong emotions and traumatic experiences. It is undoubtedly a highly absorbent stone, which needs to be cleansed frequently, more than the others, so it can release the low energy it has absorbed.

The oracle: *My female energy leads you back to yourself, to the anger that inflames you and childhood stories that today hold you back. Find yourself again; accept yourself for who you truly are inside!*

Emerald

Chakra:
Heart Chakra / *Anahata*

Color:
Green

Keyword:
Balance

This stone is traditionally tied to the magic of love and romanticism. Emerald is the queen stone of the heart chakra. Thanks to its action, the fourth chakra can be harmonized to restore balance and activated to reach stabilization. This wonderful stone is connected to the inner garden, the immense nourishing emotional capacity that the heart possesses by nature.

The oracle: *Behind the shine, I can bring you the strength of a heart able to process the greatest sorrows, the saddest memories. Are you listening to yourself enough? Have you come to terms with your power?*

Green Aventurine

Chakra:
Heart Chakra / *Anahata*

Color:
Green

Keyword:
Release

Green aventurine helps melt emotions and let go of old patterns that are no longer needed. Being a green-colored stone, it promotes the processing of emotions in general, prompting proper functioning of the heart chakra. This quartz helps us focus on the fact that the heart is the center of everything, and that love can melt away any fears or problems. It reminds us that our actions toward others can, sooner or later, affect us.

The oracle: *I dissolve that pain you feel in your heart, that symbol of inability to process, to let flow. But first look at yourself; I'll help you accept your responsibilities. Free your heart; it will make you lighter!*

Lapis Lazuli

Chakra:
Throat Chakra / *Vishuddha*

Color:
Blue

Keyword:
Communication

Intense blue in color with gold-colored specks of pyrite, it reminds us of a bright starry sky. It works mainly on communicative traits. It connects us with deep feelings, pushing us to transmit them through our most evolved part. Lapis lazuli expresses its drive through freedom of expression, but also physical movement. It promotes creativity and instills confidence in one's intuition. Lapis lazuli urges us to search for our untapped gifts.

The oracle: *It is difficult to talk about those things hiding in the depths; they are scary, but they will become gold. I connect to your wise part, which will help your communication, so I can change the outcome.*

Sodalite

Chakra:
Throat Chakra / *Vishuddha*

Color:
Blue

Keyword:
Discernment

Sodalite brings its intense blue color to calm furious rage, offering us the key to expressing it in a productive and nondestructive way and pushing us to reflect. It stimulates the functioning of the throat chakra, located in the back at the base of the neck, which oversees insights, helping us recognize and then fully understand how to resolve the problem in question.

The oracle: *You're unsure how to communicate, but I will help you. Do not fear, it may not be complete peace, but I will bring you insight that cannot be undone.*

Blue Chalcedony

Chakra:
Throat Chakra / *Vishuddha*

Color:
Blue

Keyword:
Emotions

Coming across a transparent blue chalcedony is like putting your head underwater and admiring the depths of the sea with its blurred contours. This variety of quartz precisely transmits the ability of water to flow, especially when we need to meet our emotions. It facilitates those tears that have not flowed for a long time and helps to relieve the emotional pressure that would otherwise cause damage to the inside of our body.

The oracle: *Look at me carefully, in me you will find the waves of the sea. I push your emotions out; let them go, freeing yourself from that burden that otherwise risks drowning you.*

Aquamarine

Chakra:
Throat Chakra / *Vishuddha*

Color:
Light blue

Keyword:
Everything is clearer

Aquamarine is known for its intense color, typical of the water element. The influence of this stone is clarity of vision, within us and the outside world. It exalts our sensitive side, which activates the subtle sight governed by the sixth chakra, the third eye. It encourages us to regain the enthusiasm we lost after negative experiences and to embrace the joy of flying high to explore the world inside and outside of us.

The oracle: *I can help you see future events, even from far away, so you can decide how to deal with them or avoid them. Joy will return to your heart, the beauty that you had forgotten will return.*

Angelite

Chakra:
Throat Chakra / *Vishuddha*

Color:
Light blue

Keyword:
Calm

Angelite influences the subtle and spiritual sphere more than the physical one. Its cerulean blue color immediately invokes a feeling of calm. It exercises its qualities on the communicative level, succeeding in lowering aggressiveness during a discussion. It facilitates access to guides and angels; in fact, the name of the stone comes from them. Wearing angelite offers a peaceful effect that isn't easily undermined by external events.

The oracle: *Though I cannot guarantee joy, I show you the road. From up here, where the divine order comes to my aid, we move through the dense energies of the earth together. No, you are not alone: wear me to perceive it.*

Azurite

Chakra:
Throat Chakra / *Vishuddha* and Third Eye Chakra / *Ajna*

Color:
Blue

Keyword:
Vision

Azurite is a magnificent stone that affects two different chakras: the fifth and sixth. Its work on the throat chakra is about communication. Azurite pushes us to communicate exactly what we think. On the sixth chakra, it performs a unique job in helping us see the subtle reality. In fact, it tends to lift the veils of previous incarnations, allowing us to glimpse our past lives and often helping us to grasp the meaning of the present incarnation in order to identify what we have inherited.

The oracle: *I strongly urge you to remember and see what is useful to you from the past. Are you ready to see?*

Sugilite

Chakra:
Third Eye Chakra / *Ajna*

Color:
Purple

Keyword:
Connection

Rare sugilite, with its intense purple, offers help to the mechanisms that connect us with the universe. Wearing it, in fact, heightens the senses, expanding them to their maximum potential. It is a stone that balances the physical energy with the etheric (the subtlest) energy, integrating them, and allows us to connect to the highest part of the universe, such as the spiritual guides and higher orders.

The oracle: *I help you harmonize the subtle bodies, your way of connecting upward, regrouping your energies, and preparing you for the new.*

Purple Fluorite

Chakra:
Third Eye Chakra / *Ajna*

Color:
Purple

Keyword:
Equilibrium

The beautiful purple fluorite increases the ability to receive impressions from the physical world and, above all, the spiritual world. It urges us to navigate below the conscious level to explore emotions that, if listened to, could prove to be evolutionary, keys to an important turning point in our lives. Fluorite works on the spiritual side with the intention of helping us turn inward, searching our depths for the spiritual being within us.

The oracle: *The clarity of the world, this is what I bring to you. I help you unravel what is imagined from what is real, and hold it back. Search the sky, the cosmos. Find it within you!*

Amethyst

Chakra:
Third Eye Chakra / *Ajna*

Color:
Purple

Keyword:
See

Amethyst teaches us that what we see is almost never as it seems, that behind every fact of life is an evolutionary explanation. The third eye, or the sixth energy point, benefits significantly from amethyst, which helps emphasize sight, hearing, and subtle sensations in general. Dream activity is enhanced, and the stone helps you remember dreams and find the message offered for evolutionary purposes.

The oracle: *Look inside yourself at the many things to discover and evaluate. With new clarity, look outward, at a world that until today you have not seen.*

Ametrine

Chakra:
Third Eye Chakra / *Ajna*

Colors:
Purple and yellow

Keyword:
Stability

Ametrine quartz comes from the fusion, or the heating, of an amethyst, which also absorbs the yellow of citrine. It is an interesting stone for balancing our sensitive side and making it stronger. In short, this quartz helps balance male and female energies. It brings more rationality where we have an excess of spirituality because this tends to make us perceive things as elusive, creating a sense of frustration in the long term.

The oracle: *I bring lucidity when emotions take over. I am spirit when your ego is extroverted, leading you off of your path. Put spirit at the service of your ego!*

Magnesite

Chakra:
Crown Chakra / *Sahasrara*

Color:
White

Keyword:
Purification

This stone appears as a clustered shape of white color. Similar to a pencil eraser, magnesite is a kind of eraser that is used on auric bodies to absorb dissonant energies. In particular, it is used at the end of a crystal therapy session to absorb low energy that has moved from the subtle bodies to the surface.

The oracle: *I clean your first body, the etheric one, like an eraser on your aura; I lighten your electric charge. I absorb the tension so you can relax. Clean up and leave to me what you no longer need.*

White Onyx

Chakra:
Crown Chakra / *Sahasrara*

Color:
White

Keyword:
Equilibrium

White Onyx is responsible for bringing light by channeling it from the seventh chakra to the lower chakras. Its maximum usefulness is expressed on those who have a particularly sensitive, emotional, and weak physicality and energy structure, who struggle to stay rooted to the ground, and on those who tend to take refuge in the sky to escape from ordinary occupational problems.

The oracle: *I must remind you that before reaching the spirit I must bring the spirit into the matter. I help you to love the earth with its difficulties, to find light even in the most difficult events.*

Moonstone

Chakra:
Crown Chakra / *Sahasrara*

Color:
Milky white

Keyword:
Sensitivity

Moonstone can be placed upon two areas of the body: the root chakra and the third eye. It is good to understand the archetype of the moon, that of femininity and sensitivity. Placed on the third eye, the stone enhances intuitiveness and clairvoyance, increasing subtle sight to carry out meditation or healing work. This crystal brings joy by working on the emergence and acceptance of one's feminine aspects.

The oracle: *I lead you to a clear vision, inside and outside of you. I am the feminine energy that teaches you to receive and transform.*

Selenite

Chakra:
Crown Chakra / *Sahasrara*

Color:
White

Keyword:
Awakening

Selenite owes its name to its resemblance to the moon, which does a very similar job reflecting light rays and creating fascinating reflections. Selenite brings us closer to our divine side, which we will reach by evolving into different incarnations. To become divine beings, slowly detaching ourselves from the density of human life, is what selenite asks of us.

The oracle: *I bring light where your darkness creates disorder. If you find me on your path, it is like a godsend. Look for things to change about yourself. I'll help you see them.*

Hyaline Quartz

Chakra:
Crown Chakra / *Sahasrara*

Color:
Transparent

Keyword:
Connect

This crystal naturally has a single tip (single termination) or double tip (double termination). With this crystal, we can amplify our own frequencies by raising them up, helping us overcome various dysfunctional behavioral issues by first understanding them. It can be used throughout the body and is particularly effective on the seventh chakra, the center of our connection with our spiritual side.

The oracle: *Lemuria and Atlantis knew me well. I empower your being. I detoxify lost souls. I am light made matter. Study the laws of the cosmos. Raise your frequencies.*

First Chakra

Chakra:
Root Chakra / *Muladhara*

Colors:
Red or black / red in activation, black in rooting

Keywords:
I exist

The first chakra is connected to the element Earth. Here we find all the basic principles essential to life, such as eating, sleeping and reproducing. This chakra embodies the principle of survival and regeneration of the species. The difference between the two principles—active and receptive—is contained in the first chakra. The reproductive glands associated with the chakra fulfill the principle of creation.

The oracle: *Rooted with your feet on the ground, only in this way can you exist! I am in contact with the basic emotions, with the fire that burns with passion. Through earthly experiences you evolve, finding solutions.*

Second Chakra

Chakra:
Sacral Chakra / *Svadhisthana*

Color:
Bright orange

Keywords:
I feel

Management of our feminine aspects, processing of emotions, and inner listening are found in the second chakra. Thanks to Svadhisthana, the animal and primitive nature of reproductive sexuality of the first chakra gives way to emotions and feelings, and the animal being is transformed into a higher being, which associates sexual union with the word "love." The true union of instinct and emotion takes place in this energy center.

The oracle: *I dispense feminine energy that welcomes, feels, and transforms, and that magically transmutes sex into love. I digest life and allow you to evolve!*

Third Chakra

Chakra:
Solar Plexus Chakra / *Manipura*

Color:
Golden yellow

Keywords:
I am

The third chakra is connected to the male principle, characterized by an inclination to being active, linked to construction and destruction. Manipura is an expression of personal power that is internalized and processed in the second chakra and then made available as personality to be used in the world. This energy center gives you the ability to manifest your power, which is initially internal, so that you can achieve personal fulfillment.

The oracle: *I am the ego that builds, and I am the same ego but convoluted—that destroys. Shine, build, place yourself at the service of the cosmos.*

Fourth Chakra

Chakra:
Heart Chakra / *Anahata*

Colors:
Emerald green or bright pink

Keywords:
I love

There are different types of love. The one Anahata refers to is the fusion of animalistic love and intellectual love, the cosmic love that puts us on Earth in order to evolve through emotions. The heart chakra performs two predominant activities: the transformation of human emotions, which are thinned and manifested inside and outside of us; and affectionate support in life's emotionally challenging moments.

The oracle: *I teach you unconditional love. I teach you to give while expecting nothing in return. I serve the heart for love, the lungs for flight, and in return I ask only that you become less animalistic.*

Fifth Chakra

Chakra:
Throat Chakra / *Vishuddha*

Color:
Starry night blue

Keywords:
I create

The fifth chakra has to do with communication and listening. It has both an external and internal dimension: external when the space outside of us is verbalized, internal when it concerns the ability to listen and communicate the messages coming from the body. It is recommended to pay close attention to what is said because it might come true. The fifth chakra has the power to manifest what we think by vocalizing it.

The oracle: *My greatest power is that of communication, followed by the power to manifest. Be careful what you ask for, as it will be given.*

Sixth Chakra

Chakra:
Third Eye Chakra / *Ajna*

Color:
Purple

Keywords:
I see

The sixth chakra is perhaps the chakra usually attributed with the most importance. It is the chakra that gives you a clear and sharp vision of your inner self. It allows you to see and perceive the subtle reality around you. It allows us to observe the movement of energy that surrounds us, to see entities and spirit guides, and it offers the possibility to interact with them in a more direct and sometimes more functional way.

The oracle: *I invite you to look inside yourself: see the things that elude you and those that need to be improved.*

Seventh Chakra

Chakra:
Crown Chakra / *Sahasrara*

Color:
Bright white

Keywords:
I exist

The seventh chakra speaks to our connection to the divine dimension, to the universe. Careful listening and observation of the cosmic rules allow us to perceive ourselves as spiritual beings, incarnating a physical body on Earth to experience an evolutionary path. If experiences, whether positive or negative, are absorbed as teachings, they allow us to take steps forward into a deeper understanding of life.

The oracle: *The energy of creation flows through me, nourishing you, bringing you closer to the cosmos. Did you know that the brain is just the servant of the highest subtle bodies?*

Stone Cleansing

Helping card

To be clean means to be free and lighter. It is important that the environment in which you move and the objects you meet are not loaded with the heavy energies that derive from previous uses—yours or of others—so you avoid absorbing them yourself. To transform the energy of stones or other objects from heavy to light, place them on an amethyst druse for 72 hours, away from direct sunlight. You can also use the druse to cleanse the energy in an environment.

The oracle: *Pay attention to the environment and the objects you come in contact with: do they lighten or burden your energy?*

Aura Cleansing

Helping card

Subtle bodies need cleansing. Crowded or dirty places, closed environments and air conditioning, electromagnetic pollution and tensions weigh down the auric layers, mainly the etheric and the emotional. Thus, through etheric tears, the development of energetic parasites is likely. Thorough cleansing favors the removal of unwanted guests, restoring energy and clarity.

The oracle: *It's time to think about the integrity of your aura—feel it, focus. What can you do to lighten yourself from the inside?*

Messages

Helping card

Are you listening to yourself? If you want to receive messages from the cosmos or from your guides, you need to pay attention to yourself. Stop and find precious moments of silence in which to close your eyes and listen. You can also ask for messages to be conveyed to you in other ways. Messages can often come through daily signs, repetitive numbers, books, or meetings. Look around you: there is no such thing as chance, just signs through which the cosmos communicates with human beings.

The oracle: *If you want to access the messages of the cosmos, all you have to do is ask.*

Energy Vampire

Helping card
....

There are times when your personal energy is low and you need to recharge. Some choose to suck energy from the vibrational field of close by people. Headache, limp legs, fatigue, desire to sleep, nausea—these are the signs of someone being drained of their energy. Do you feel drained by some people? Are you going through a moment of fatigue and vampirizing others? Or maybe it's your ordinary habit?

The oracle: *Find or protect the authentic source of your energy. A red jasper in the left pocket will help you either way.*

Feminine Principle

Helping card

The feminine principle belongs to both women and men. This quality concerns receptivity: the ability to welcome impressions, emotions, an event within oneself, and then have the capacity to transform them and bring life to something new. To do so, you must listen to yourself.

The oracle: *In a hurry? Slow down, listen to your little inner voice. What is the cosmos asking of you that you are perhaps trying to avoid hearing? Are you transforming that emotion, even if it is difficult to do so? Are you welcoming it?*

Masculine Principle

Helping card

This principle is based on action, both for women and for men. Being an active participant in the world, moving within the space. However, if you do not focus your feminine part, you risk releasing energy as a destructive fury. The masculine principle does not want to dominate, but rather protect, build, and put itself at the service of the world and not just of itself.

The oracle: *Where are you heading right now? Is your ego taking over? What do you do to put yourself at the service of the world? Are you giving something of yourself?*

LUCA APICELLA

Since childhood, Luca has been attracted to nature and the energy that comes from the Earth. This call led him to study Reiki, starting a wonderful journey that would introduce him to naturopathy and bionatural healing. Over the years, he has added crystal therapy and other energy disciplines to his list of healing modalities, and the subject of his teaching and education. Since 2021, he has been an expert facilitator in forest medicine (shinrin-yoku) and counselor in psychosomatic therapy.

In his in-person and online courses, he combines his training with being in nature and forests, knowing that coming into contact with our beloved trees and nature from which we come can make a difference over a short period of time.

ALESSANDRA DE CRISTOFARO

Alessandra is an illustrator for magazines, communication agencies, and international publishing houses. Her work is inspired by her holistic and spiritual interests and is marked by her focus on the relationship between the interior and exterior worlds, which is expressed through a dreamlike and surreal atmosphere, developed from a "pop" perspective.